SENSIBLE SENSES
SONGS OF SOLILOQUY

SARVESH NIKUMBH

Copyright © Sarvesh Nikumbh
All Rights Reserved.

ISBN 978-1-63781-395-9

This book has been published with all efforts taken to make the material error-free after the consent of the author. However, the author and the publisher do not assume and hereby disclaim any liability to any party for any loss, damage, or disruption caused by errors or omissions, whether such errors or omissions result from negligence, accident, or any other cause.

While every effort has been made to avoid any mistake or omission, this publication is being sold on the condition and understanding that neither the author nor the publishers or printers would be liable in any manner to any person by reason of any mistake or omission in this publication or for any action taken or omitted to be taken or advice rendered or accepted on the basis of this work. For any defect in printing or binding the publishers will be liable only to replace the defective copy by another copy of this work then available.

Dedicated to My Mother

Dedicated to My father

Dedicated to My Brother

Contents

Part 1

1. Think, Just Think...	3
2. Me	4
3. The Linguistic Mind	5
4. The Illusion	6
5. The Corruption	8
6. The Dual Character Within	9
7. Looking From Above	11
8. People With Bad Speech	12
9. Regret No More!	13
10. The Truth Of Failure	15

Part 2

11. O' Friend	19
12. I Hear A Bee…	21
13. Observing It!	22
14. Flow With Life	24
15. The Control	26
16. Soliloquy For Reality	27
17. A Simple Solution	28
18. The Opposite Nature-1	30
19. All Of It	31
20. As You Are!	33

Part 3

21. There I Sit	37

Contents

22. The Rain	38
23. Wedding	39
24. The Choice	41
25. Judgment	43
26. The Opposite Nature-2	45
27. A Match For You	46
28. Conquering Fear	47
29. Laying Grounds	48
30. Goodbye Believers!	50

Carry your peace,

Don't let it control you,

Honour your pain,

Don't let it ruin you!

Part 1

1. Think, Just Think...

Higher in the sky,

Deeper in the mine,

Clashes of thunder die

And earthquakes lie…

The wonderful dreams of a boy

Demolished by his own sky,

The concurrence of all phases in his mind

Took him to the marvelous sky…

Since he also got that second eye,

To watch beyond the darker lie,

Contrasting to the spectacular flight,

The flame of brilliance vanished in the mine.

2. Me

I am so used to pain now,
That pain is what entertains me!

I am so used to healing now,
That healings are my best friends!

I am so used to smile now,
That smiling is what makes my face my own!

I am so used to shy now,
That shyness is what defines my emotions!

I am so used to be humble now,
That being humble is what I do when I quarrel!

I am so used to soliloquy now,
That my words are what makes me 'Me'.

3. The Linguistic Mind

Causing me to rhyme,
Causing me to whine,
This my love, My English,
Is it any wine?

Books are where I step-in,
Books are where I peep-in,
Language is so ingrained within,
Whenever I see its beauty,
My heart starts beating.

Weeping, whipping,
Leaping, peeping,
And dreaming about it,
That's the way,
My mind behaves,
So naive it may be,
So beautifully it's shaping!

4. The Illusion

Write about my suffering,
Write about my plight,
There is nothing wrong with it,
There is nothing right.

It aches my eyes,
When I see a disturbing sight,
There is always dark,
And there is always light.

Often I feel,
The days are too bright,
They are either murky,
Or bright as yellow and white.

Simple mistake often bring on fights,
Why hurt yourself in a fight?
Enemy can assault you,
But you can choose to quite.

Life is a cake of sweets,
Or is it just a sweet bite?
Sorrow is an illusion,
It's never built to heights!

5. The Corruption

Last Night an insect bit me,
I don't know which kind it was!
But a round red blister,
As a tiny hill , appeared on my skin.

That maybe a real insect,
With real consequences,
What about those insects,
Which crawl through my mind?

Mind has it's own variety maybe,
What about the remaining body?
Heart has it's own allegiance,
Is love one of them?

Sometimes insects can crawl,
From your mind and heart,
To other body parts,
But they should not corrupt more!

6. The Dual Character within

Relief isn't a choice,
If you can't realize its value,
Peace within you,
Can be found instantly!

Tell me why you worry,
I shall answer you the cause,
But not the right one,
Rather confusing you a lot!

Call me your mate
Or call me your enemy,
I will trick and tease you,
Unless you keep quiet!

Deal with your misery,
Deal with your wounds,
Everything is a question,
So stop answering it loud!

SENSIBLE SENSES

Carry your peace,
Don't let it control you,
Honour your pain,
Don't let it ruin you!

Apply little logic,
Where you fail to be sensitive,
Claim your health,
Over the helpless occasions!

7. Looking from Above

Standing on a cliff,
Pinnacle of the world,
Walked my way up, a Ranger aloof,
Not very young and not too old!

Startled with questions,
Befuddled with myself,
Finding my colleague within me,
Got so much to ralph!

Rather Hiding at this place,
From that puzzling maze,
Where Money is the only craze,
And harmful greed lays!

Harsh it may sound,
But I see a lot of bloodhound,
Like those people are spellbound,
who can not even expound!

8. People with Bad Speech

Windows made of glasses not woods,
Such as a heart of of tissues not goods,
What shape of your mouth,
Which can attack these hearts,
Wide it goes, crushing all the muscles,
Cracking all over, and again crushing through souls!
Glideth blood, pumping thy veins,
Pumping thy heartbeats, through rigorous train of rafts!
Raging all over, all the bodies that surround this waste of energy;
Life is wasted in these speeches,
Lower the quality of words,
Degrading everyone with thyself!

9. Regret no more!

To fall in love is like a dream,
To fall for life is relatively easy,
To get a job is like a dream,
To earn money is relatively easy,
But it is not!
Like the way it sound so easy,
But to say it, may sound so lazy!

To get what you need is what it's about,
To get what you want is not so easy!
To have what you need,
Is it all worth it?
And does other Things not count?
Something right, something precise,
Something crazy to suit me,
And something wide, something big
For my mind!
To know what I want
Others may always deny,
I make myself busy to have that,
To try that I should pay for it so hard!

Shot the ball in the goal,
Till it reach the target hole,
Make every effort,
Give all your focus it wants!
All the night that you dream,
And everyday you think it bad,
And remember,
you will hate yourself
if you loose it all!!!

10. The Truth of Failure

Beneath the unimaginable powers,
What one has got, is the control,
If the one can monitor them,
Then the one is independent and can do anything.

Beneath that unforgivable anger,
The one has got the control to forget,
If that one is independent of dudgeon
and can be cooled easily!

Beneath the unforgettable sorrow,
That one has got the things,
Which makes him cheerful,
If the one can concentrate on those things,
Then he is independent of the peaks of sorrow,
no matter how high the peaks are,
they can be destroyed by the one…

But it reminds us about one of the exceptions of nature,
And his subconscious tells him that it is impossible,
Where all turns WORTHLESS!

Part 2

11. O' Friend

Dear, Dear Friend,
Help me and teach me to pray,
Gather with me,
Make me something to say,
Lot in the nature,
Charming, detenting, everything is in the way.
If you are my friend,
Don't care whatever it may!
Lot to worry, lot to say,
Lot to learn, lot is away,
Why does this happen with me again and again,
Sometimes for now,
Sometimes for then,
This my phren is killed in pain.
The relief comes when,
The flowers blossom,
And the birds rise again,
While'st the clouds fade away,
After the rain.
Come with me,
With no shame,
Enjoy the joyous,
Resist the pain,

Let's partner ourselves,
It is time to gain again!

12. I hear a bee…

I hear a bee humming in my ear,
Sometimes when I feel pale,
It blocks the surroundings,
Gives me a feeling of detachment

I hear another bee humming in my ear,
Sometimes when I am too happy,
It tells me that the air is sweet than ever,
Gives me a feeling of oneness

I hear a bee different than others,
Sometimes When I am too excited,
It takes me to another dimension of life,
Where I feel like I own everything!

One day I thought,
Am I the master of these bees?
Or a slave to their presence?
And realised that, they are friends with my emotions,
They simply accompany me as per my emotions!

13. Observing It!

Racing through my heart
And racing through my mind
Racing through the world
Racing through all the mankind.

This mind, this heart
Linked together, feeling the air
Feeling life all the way
Around the world.

Touching every face,
Touching every mind,
Spiritual world I see
Stealing from the light.
Wonders everywhere
Spreading day and night
Shall I stop imagining,
Such a handsome plight?

Is it east or west?
Not a dirty quest,
Travelling is never a waste,
Always kind of haste!

But imagine travelling
Is a Spiritual quest,
Staying at your nest,
Feeling everything best!

14. Flow With Life

Drinking water keeps you hydrated,
Will worrying make you a greatest thinker?
Eating a lot bring weight to you,
Will talking too much reduce your lungs?

Try to have some air,
Inhaling it may bring more peace,
But can you taste it?
And so that you never starve!

While we work for living,
Work for peace too!
And while we pray,
Don't kill yourself dreaming!

Till the next breathe,
The last one fades,
And till the next life,
This one ends!

Dont wait for goals to fulfill,
Keep in control the wheel of joy,
Ride with such enthusiasm,
That it will drive you to eternity!

15. The Control

Rally of the masses,
Gathers only for injustice,
Creeping diaries of their walks,
Shape their woe's classes.

Trimming the unlawful crimes,
Will the society be better?
Justice is not a fruit of fight,
It is a truth of warriors!

Live your life,
Without harm for anyone,
Claim your rewards,
Without injustice to yourself!

Grab those celebrations;
Keep them in a corner of your mind,
So that no thief can steal them,
While you still can rewind!

16. Soliloquy for Reality

Lucky are those who are destined to die,
Lucky are those who get to live,
Terrible tragedies everywhere,
For those who try to love

Disastrous adobes are everywhere
For those who struggle always
Lamentations for every emotion
Lamentations with fake covers to books.

Torn up pages for all the needy readers
And unwashed clothes for those hungry workers,
Tragic deaths are common,
Tragic births are not that rare!

Failure for life and failure for love,
Incarnations for few and gifts for all,
But To know how they will shape us,
And being wise to understand is Ecstatic.

17. A Simple Solution

Why are there wrinkles on your face?
Why are there worries in the world?
Are these the related terms to misery?
Or is it ageing paired with misery?

Normally what we see is beautiful,
About nature and about our faces,
But when our faces look pale,
Do they look same as if experiencing pleasure?

A baby is always innocent,
And always adorable,
If smiling, he seems to own the world,
If crying, it seems the world has crashed down.

Rather we believe having a companion,
Who relieves us of our stress,
Is it necessary to have one?
Don't you have yourself to make you happy?

Sit straight with eyes closed,
And focus on past pleasure moments,
Can you see how you felt at that time?
Experience it again and again, you have now a way to feel happy anytime!

18. The Opposite Nature-1

Too worthy, too slow
Too bluff to know,
The sacred for nothing
But innocent with glow!
Turtle we say it,
Calmness it show.

Too Fast, too fleet,
Too high to fly,
The scary for nothing,
But always in the sky!
Eagle we say it,
Smart always thy…

19. All Of It

Life comes to those,
who care to invite it,
Shine comes to those,
who want to lighten it.

Whenever you will avoid,
to lift the heavy weight,
you will loose the chance;
to strengthen thy muscles.

The desire you keep,
To take some effort,
Can uplift your will,
To become 'Brave'!

Running and hiding,
from responsibilities you are given,
will shut every door
one day; I bet

No direction, if you ignore
The road of light,
And no teacher can save you,
Blur dreams, less bright!

Love comes to those,
Who care to care,
And compassion comes to those,
Who want it to be shared!

Likewise love your path of dreams,
Be compassionate by every means,
Care for yourself and everyone,
Once you seek the bliss then the anguish is done.

20. As you are!

If future is making no sense,
When you call it up,
Talk it up freely,
It won't let you know 'what is it?',
It won't come down!

Sprung up in the past,
You will come to know that,
Nothing is exact as you thought,
Hence chill it down,
And catch the brisk and dawn!

Claim what you seek,
Play what you dream,
Change what you see,
And Don't be mean!

Life has become a Fantasy,
And no demon in a dream,
Beat it up,
live it up,
swag in your style!

Part 3

21. There I sit

I packed my sack,
And took my heaven,
What do you think?
"How is that heaven?"
What I implied was that,
My books are my heaven!

Am I so happy,
To look at those books?
In my everyday seat
In left corner below the misc hooks!

That corner was not any ordinary one,
It took me to the lives of great people,
showed me lives of great fictional characters,
gave me some beautiful memories with them,
sometimes I cried for them,
and at times celebrated with them!

22. The Rain

Dirty the mud,
muddy the flood,
little drops of pearls,
starting their journey,
departure from home cloud,
undefined their fate,
with the thunders roaring aloud.

Tiny, round, array of dots,
The pearls of water,
They are so clean,
Shining with proud.

First array has just landed safely,
the magic smell of their hug to the the land,
now their beautiful excursion to this heaven,
fresh and marvelous, here is the Rainy season.

23. Wedding

Dancing people down the hall,
What a beauty there in the middle,
Classic it may sound,
Glamour all it is!

Shining faces with pleasure,
Smiling ladies in the corner,
Blind eyes of men,
And everything so clear.

Music playing slow but loud,
Dancers as if waves,
With rhythm and moves,
Trading on the rollers!

Here's the bride and groom,
They are happy but mute,
Smiling both with blissful evening,
What lay ahead do they know?

Centre of attention,
Floating from ladies,
To the random dancers,
Who look handsome but with pride!

24. The Choice

Lame is the destiny,
Of whom the ambition is hollow!
Shame is the longing,
Of whom the bullying is business!

Fame is the destiny,
Of whom longing is no more!
Fulfilled ambitions with grace,
For them who bullies no one!

Charm is the destiny,
Of whom compassion is a jewel,
A jewel with inner beauty,
Attracting every human!

Crime is the destiny
Of whom greed is ingrained,
Rude behaviour and unhealthy life,
Is their daily routine!

What to be? And how to be?
This is the choice you make,
Embrace happiness with
The whole of it's ambit.

25. Judgment

Blood is red,
Body isn't,
Hairs are black,
Mind isn't!

We see surfaces,
Not the cores!
We judge by looks,
And with fore!

Life is tricky,
As we all are,
We fight each other,
Like it's a war!

Look up the sky,
With eyes open wide,
Brighter but why?
So we can't hide!

Everything is clear,
As bright days,
But with frightful fear,
Darkness lays some rays!

26. The Opposite Nature-2

Clay made stiff,
Statues made along,
Tree with a leaf,
Say it so-long!

Statues took shapes,
And started a new life,
Tree is dying as apes,
Cut by a long big knife!

Statues will earn,
Changing homes
Tree will burn,
Turning into coals!

Statues of clay,
Respected for art,
Tree gave us this day,
It has ended in dirt!

27. A Match for You

Some of the feelings can't be expressed with words,
Some of them can only be expressed with words,
Some of them can't be tasted on the way,
When one of then wins,
and other withdraws,
When Excuse comes for a refuge,
And well planned tragedy scatters all around,
Remember you are your only friend,
To rejoice life,
Again with yourself!

28. Conquering Fear

O' that fear,
Damn! it was haunting me all along,
Forgetting myself, which is wrong,
Sentencing myself to become strong,
Suffering is neither short nor too long!

Fear for suffering is the worst of all,
Call it a curse or call it a maul,
Hide your worries and take a stroll,
Lock them in coffin, cover it with a pall!

29. Laying grounds

I want something that would peel the skin,

I want something that would heal a kill,

I want to gift humanity the feeling of loneliness,

Of how unfortunate one could feel in this world!

Its a daunting task, to live life,

As if walking through the rocks!

I want to Engage them to believe in fate!

how happy one could get without any hate!

And how sad one could get if he is fogotten by his mates!

The only answer I found till now,

Is only producing many more questions,

Till I discover one converging thought for it all,

I will not rest in peace!

30. Goodbye Believers!

Rolling down my eyes,
The subtle pain of cries,
Shameless and wise,
Rise above it; rise!

Cold with shivers,
Still with tears,
Goodbye believers,
I am pulling the levers!

Call me day,
Call me night,
Call me a ray,
Or Call me to light!

Smile, if you can't,
Coz That's what I want,
Stopping, you shan't,
Until you die that'll haunt!

One way is up,
Other one comes down,
Don't you give up,
We want the crown!

Tales even in the shadows,
Cracking me all over,
Developing me and my vows,
Increasing my power!

www.ingramcontent.com/pod-product-compliance
Lightning Source LLC
LaVergne TN
LVHW042001060526
838200LV00041B/1825